THE ODD ONE OUT

a spotting book

Britta Teckentrup

"Hello! Good morning!"
a flock of birds tweet.
As the sun rises,
they're ready to eat.

Looking for something
that wriggles and squirms,
which little bird finds
a pink juicy worm?

As moonlight replaces
the rays of the sun,
a cauldron of bats
come out looking for fun.

Stretching their wings,
they take to the skies –
but which of them still
hasn't opened its eyes?

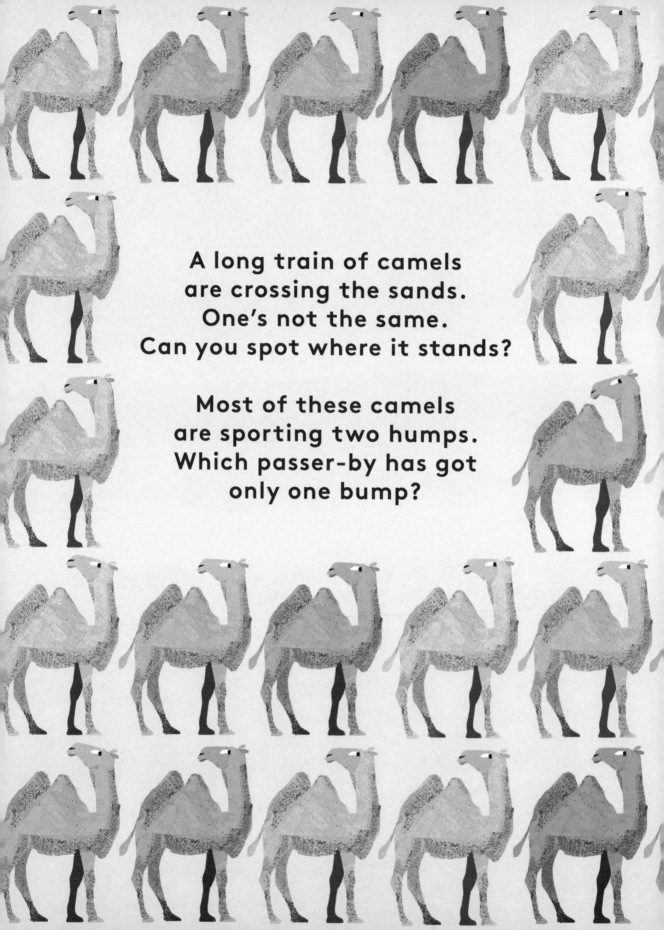

A long train of camels
are crossing the sands.
One's not the same.
Can you spot where it stands?

Most of these camels
are sporting two humps.
Which passer-by has got
only one bump?

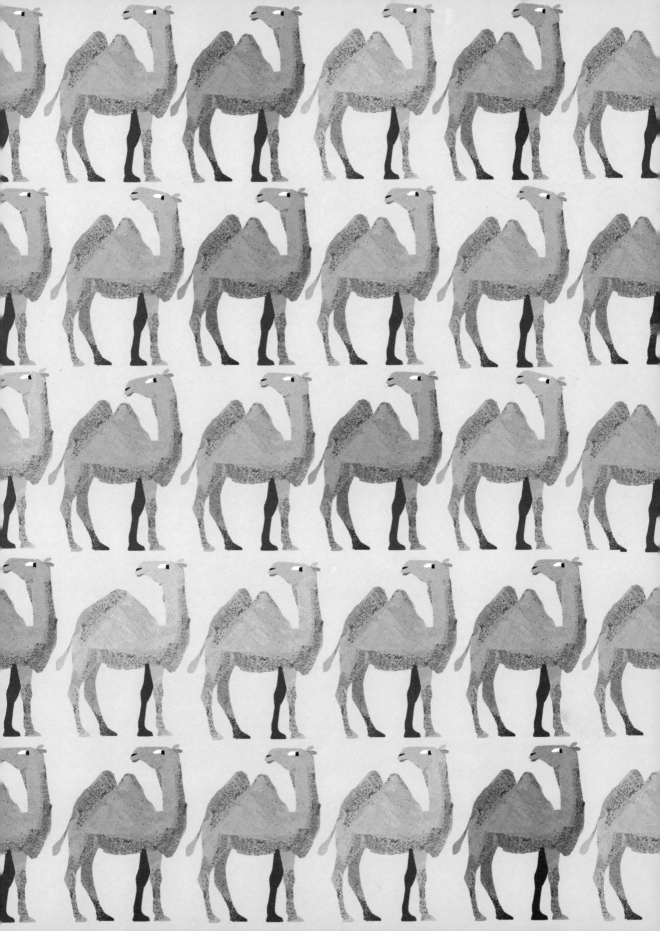

A pod of seals bark,
calling out for their dinner.
Who gets the first fish?
Can you spot the winner?

"Me next! It is mine!"
each seal loudly cries,
but which one's already
chewing its prize?

A creep of fine tortoises
slowly pass by.
Watching the birds,
they look up at the sky.

Most of them smile,
but one's frightened instead.
Which one is scared
and has hidden its head?

A wobble of ostriches
stand tall and proud,
forming a handsome
and feathery crowd.

As these fine birds
stop to gather around,
which of them pecks
at a seed on the ground?

A sleuth of plump pandas
have put on a show,
wobbling their bellies
as white as the snow.

Jumping and jigging
to entertain you,
which of the pandas
has lost its bamboo?

A cartload of monkeys
spin round and around.
Which took a tumble
and fell to the ground?

Here is a clue
as to who it could be:
which one has bandaged
its arm and its knee?

A crash full of rhinos
is coming this way.
With a stamp and a snort,
they've been walking all day.

Feeling weak-kneed as
its friends huff and frown,
which little rhino
sits wearily down?

A stand of flamingos
look pretty in pink.
Peering up coyly,
they flutter and wink.

As they stand preening
their feathers with care,
which of them's lifting
their leg in the air?

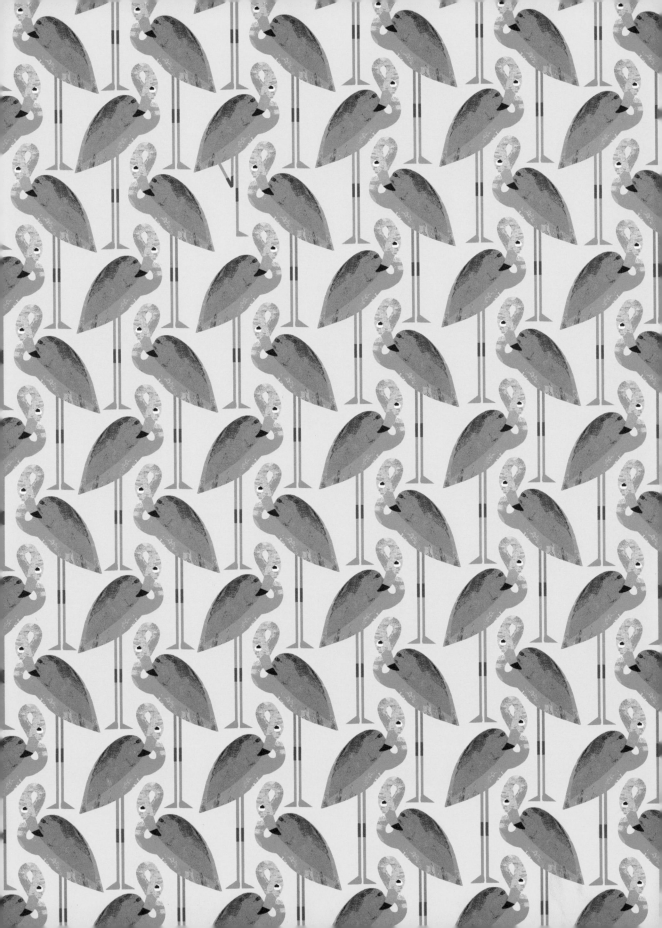

A dazzling shoal
of fish in the sea
are keeping a secret –
but what could it be?

A shy little shrimp swims
with fish on all sides
to stay out of sight –
can you spot where it hides?

A lemur troop sit
with their tails long and striped.
Startled, together
they look up in fright.

Stopping and staring,
they strike the same pose,
but which is cross-eyed
as it looks at its nose?

Elegant penguins
stand round in a huddle.
All black and white,
they are easy to muddle!

One has a secret
stowed under its wing.
Who is protecting
a little fledgling?

A rabble of colourful,
bright butterflies
emerge from cocoons
and take off for the skies.

One caterpillar's
still waiting, it seems.
But can he be found
as he looks up and dreams?

Congratulations!
You've challenged your eyes!
And here we have hidden
one final surprise.

This book has been filled with
these creatures throughout...
But one here is new!
Who's our last odd one out?

BIG PICTURE PRESS
www.bigpicturepress.net

First published in the UK and Australia in 2014 by Big Picture Press,
an imprint of The Templar Company Limited,
Deepdene Lodge, Deepdene Avenue, Dorking, Surrey, RH5 4AT, UK
www.templarco.co.uk

ISBN 978-1-84877-351-6

Printed in China

This book was typeset in Brown.
The illustrations were created digitally.

Edited by Jenny Broom
Designed by Andy Mansfield

For Vincent – B.T.